You Took My Chakras

Michele Prudlo

Presentation by *BookLeaf Publishing*

Web: www.bookleafpub.com

E-mail: info@bookleafpub.com

ISBN: 9789357612913

First edition 2022

*I want to dedicate this book to every lover
out here. People that have loved, and
continue to, regardless of how much
heartache it can cause.*

ACKNOWLEDGEMENT

I would like to acknowledge the artist Ryan Johnson who was able to bring my vision into reality.

PREFACE

We all live an unbalanced life in areas we wish we weren't. Humans hurt each other so much, that it can feel like they have left us and stole our chakras. These beautiful poems are inspired by the heart chakra, which is the central chakra for love and compassion.

My First Poem For You

You stare in the sky with blank eyes just like me,
You wonder every day, who could I possibly be?
What should I become,
When should I be done?
I just want to tell you that your life has yet to
begin!
I don't care about your past,
How long your relationships last.
All I know is that with you,
Everything seems new.
Not that the old bothers me,
But who is she?
Who is the one that hurt you,
Where could I take you to?
Take you to a place to feel safe,
I don't want you hiding in a cave.
I can see your bright future,
I will not open up your almost healed suture.
I want you to trust me more than anyone,
Because we both know we can not trust
everyone..

Doubts

Your Words spoke Lies,
But your Eyes saw Truth.
Your Hands felt Love,
And your Feet felt Fear.
Your Brain heard Doubts,
But your Heart Knew,
That you love Her.

No matter the Lies,
Fear,
and
Doubt,
that arises every single time:

You saw her.
You felt her.
You heard her.

Nothing

Have you ever been broken up with
and then..
Started dancing..
Started playing an instrument..
Started to cook..
Started to learn to craft..
Started anything in the world;
To keep them-
From your mind..
Anything.
Absolutely just everything.
And nothing.
Is working.
At all.
Nothing

Boys Like You

Boys like you
Boys like you don't make me wait.
Boys like you don't make me pay for breakfast.
Boys like you don't leave me freezing.
Boys like you don't make me beg.
Boys like you kiss me because they desire me.
Boys like you never make me wait for a reply.
Boys like you listen to every word I say.
Boys like you aren't childish.
Boys like you always show up no matter what time it is.
Boys like you are faithful .. because boys like you are boys who see their one and only as their future, a pure diamond that's rare to find ever again. You're a man.

A Memory

5

"Yeah, they said I made a mistake.
I don't really agree.
I got to kiss you and say
"i love you.."
The way you made me feel,
Can't be a mistake,
Can't even be a lesson.
Can't possibly be karma.
It could only be a memory I'll never forget."

Compare Me To Her

"She tells you that she yearns you,
Does she even closely compare to what I mean?
Like, I absolutely can't live without you!
I need you!
Without you, I can't go on!
The kind of yearn that's not just desire.
What's beyond desire?
What I mean is,I literally can't breathe without
you."

You're Not Her

I told you,
"You're not her;
The one I would change for.
Your eyes are brown and hers are blue,
You're just not her.
The one I'd love forever,
You're just not her".

You listen to me speak,
But I said:"you're not her.
You have an accent but not the one I'm longing
for,
You're just not her.
It's cold outside and you're freezing,
But you're not the one I heat up the car seat for,
because ..
You're not her!
You expect me to open the car door, but I can't
because-
You're not her.
I'll order my meal first because only she is the
one that I'll encourage to order first, because
You're not her".

I told you:"I love you and I am sorry
But you're just not her".

Don't Pretend

I understand that you're hurt
I understand you need time

…

But I can't understand that you pretend that you
never loved me

Just A Crush

Everything looks pink,
I know, I just have a crush.
The way you talk makes me daydream,
I know I just have a crush.
Your eyes sparkle so bright,
I know I just have a crush.
I said I love you,
I know I just have a crush.
I would die for you,
I know it's just a crush.
Crash.

You Can't Change Me

You can love me,
You can put a ring on my finger,
You can even change my last name,
But you can not change the way my blood flows,
You can never change the way I love.
Even when you break me,
I'll just stop loving you.
But I'll never forget the love I can love.
I'll change my name like it's easily erased,
Like
It never even happened.

Out Of Breath

I was out of breath,
Tried to breath,
But couldn't.
I tried to hide,
Searching for a shelter,
But couldn't,
No trees to hide behind.
I was suffocating,
In the middle of the field,
Here alone now,
Without you.

Nothing Lasts Forever

Every person I've loved,
Hurt me,
Never came back.
That's how I realized,
That nothing,
Not even Love,
Ever lasts forever.

Romeo

Your words can be as beautiful as Romeos were
to Juliet,
However,
They won't mean a thing if they're not from the
one she wants to hear them from.

Agony

You don't know pain when the agony inside of you doesn't feel like the entire earth stops spinning.

Only Forever

For love you'd do anything.
So why aren't you doing everything?
It's only forever,
It would only be forever.

Party Star

You see the brightest star above,
That's the party star thereof.
That's where I'll be when I pass away,
You'll know I'm perfectly okay.
Singing and dancing and watching you from
above.
You'll feel my love.

Skeletons

They say ever rose has its thorns,
But ever human has their horns.
Evil inside of every person,
Telling lies in a different version.
No person on earth is perfect,
And we have many secrets well kept.
Skeletons hidden in every humans closet,
Wait until the day you have to put down your
deposit.

I Can But I Can't

I can eat but
I can't.
I can sleep but
I can't.
I can smile but
I can't.
I can walk but
I can't.
I can talk but
I can't.
I can think but
I can't.
I can miss you but
I can't.
Because it hurts
When I do.
I can love you
And I will,
Till I can't!